See Me For Who I Am

By Chéree L. Thomas

authorHOUSE®

AuthorHouse™
1663 Liberty Drive
Bloomington, IN 47403
www.authorhouse.com
Phone: 1-800-839-8640

First published by AuthorHouse 02/28/2011

ISBN: 978-1-4520-9032-0 (sc)
ISBN: 978-1-4520-9031-3 (dj)
ISBN: 978-1-4520-9033-7 (e)

Library of Congress Control Number: 2011900657

Printed in the United States of America

Certain stock imagery © Thinkstock.

This book is printed on acid-free paper.

Contents

Introduction

This book is intended to be utilized as a guide in the provision of services to the people of color who take the risk and ask for help. There is an emphasis on domestic and sexual violence services although; it is relevant to all service providers. The writing of this book was inspired by the many survivors of color who left agencies with a feeling of despair. In an effort to alleviate the feeling of hopelessness faced by those women, Jeanette has courageously shared her encounter with us.

Jeanette and other survivors of color have repeatedly stated that the "one size fits all" approach is rarely as beneficial as the service provider intends it to be. While services are rendered to the best of the ability of the provider, it is without regard to the person's culture. A disregard for culture portrays the service as inadequate. The person is only treated as a domestic and/or sexual violence case. Domestic and/or sexual violence is something that has happened to a person and not the definer. Ignoring this fact leads to many survivors of color to deal with trying to heal on their own.

This book seeks to eliminate some of the guessing on what to say, how to say it, or if you need to say anything at all. While this book *cannot and does not* try to cover every situation with every person of color, it will set the groundwork for working with people where they are. It will allow an appreciation for the culture that each individual brings when they walk into the door of a provider for services.

It is my intention to bridge the gap between the service provider and the person seeking services in a way that is mutually beneficial. The person seeking services will be able to receive the benefits in the way they were designed. I will share with you the journey of one woman who is a survivor of intimate partner violence and childhood sexual violence. She is now the parent of a child who is a sexual assault survivor.

Please keep in mind that each individual is unique and will bring an added dimension to the way they view themselves in their culture. It is my objective to share with you information that will be useful in every aspect of your life. None of us who are service providers live in a bubble, and are bound to come into contact with individuals whose cultural identity differs greatly from our own. Let us choose to embark on this journey for the benefit of ourselves and others.

In this book people of color are descendents of and those who self-identify as African/ African American/Black.

Culture

When we think of culture, we often limit ourselves with thought of skin color. This is both inaccurate and insulting to the person you are attempting to assist. Culture is simply the collective beliefs, values, etc. of a group of people. In other words, it is impossible to understand a person's culture based solely upon appearance. There are many blends of ethnic groups so don't be surprised when a person identifies as being in more than one.

A person's ethnic group in many cases is the beginning of their identity and not the ending. Ethnicity is one of many aspects of culture. To understand a person and their culture, one must be willing to do the work of obtaining the necessary information. In addition, the person being served is given the opportunity to inform you of their cultural identity. Culture is something that can be shared with you. Therefore, it is important to be accepting of what the survivor has shared with you regarding their culture and the role it plays in their life. Allowing the survivor to share with you their view on their culture will open the door to building trust in the relationship.

In providing services, culture has to be a consideration. Cultural insensitivity is indicative of cultural ignorance and a lack of awareness. How can you know if you are being culturally insensitive? If you have a disregard for the beliefs and values of others who don't share your belief system, you are probably exhibiting some cultural insensitivity. Your service provision does not allow room for there to be more than one way for the service to be provided.

For example, your religious practice calls for you to attend services on Sunday for an hour. Your client (in your shelter based organization) has requested to attend church all week until 11:00 p.m. You deny the request, stating curfew at 9:00 p.m. You also make the comment that you are certain that it does not take that much time for worship service. This action has alienated your client.

It is clear that you have allowed your bias to creep in and inhibit you from providing services that take into account another's culture. Your decision was not based on the needs of the client, but on your own cultural belief. If you are seeking to have a homogenous environment, then that is the way to go. If you are seeking to provide a service in an environment that is welcoming, cultural considerations will take place.

Each work environment has a culture of its own. Not allowing for variance in the environment can cause stagnation and isolation of those who do not fit the mold. Does that mean that hiring a person of color addresses the issue? Of course it does not. Being a part of a marginalized group does not translate into being an expert on all things related to the group.

For instance, you have a client that is requesting shampoo and conditioner for her natural hair (chemically untreated). You reply that you gave her shampoo upon entrance into the shelter. As the client tries to explain to you why it won't work on her hair, you interrupt and get the woman of color on staff (whose hair is chemically treated) to deal with her.

The woman of color staff person gets shampoo for the client. While the shampoo says it's for women of color it is still not what the client needs. The client accepts it as she is in need; however, both women were placed in a position of having to deal with cultural ignorance.

The woman of color service provider was chosen to be of assistance based only on her skin color. The client was given assistance that was not the most beneficial. The client will more than likely be apprehensive in asking for necessities. She does not want to feel as if she is being an imposition.

When a person of color is hired, they need to be hired for the specific skill set they bring to the organization. There is something to be said for an organization that recognizes the importance of diversity. There is even more to be said about an organization that recognizes the benefit of a positive, well-trained diverse set of employees who understand the importance of cultural competence.

Diversity impacts how a person experiences their culture. Diversity refers to the differences that make us all unique. This includes but is not limited to sex, gender, race, and religion. Our goal as service providers is to strive for cultural competence. As a service provider we strive to create an environment in which one can integrate without feeling pressure to assimilate.

Get Over It

Three of the most damaging words ever spoken to anyone who has experienced domestic or sexual violence are *"Get Over It"*. These words are often spoken in the calmest of tones as hands reach for a tissue to wash away tears. These words are often spoken by very well meaning individuals who cannot handle the truth that has just been shared with them.

At a moment when words seem to fail them and the need to fill empty space presents itself; these are the words that are spoken. It may be phrased as "move on", "it could be worse", "others have gotten pass this", "you're not the first and you won't be the last". "I know how you feel" and "I've been through the same thing" are just as harmful. Words have a lasting affect on a person and cannot be taken back once they are spoken. An opportunity to connect becomes an instance of disengagement and a countdown to ending the session. This disconnectedness has been the experience of Jeanette, a sexual assault survivor, mother and wife. She has suppressed her past. Events she could not foresee have forced her to face her history.

A Mothers Grief at Innocence Lost

Jeanette received a call from her daughter's guidance counselor. It was not unusual to hear from the guidance counselor. As most mothers' of teenagers can attest to, a call from the guidance counselor usually involves spats between friends who will once again be friends in five minutes.

However, this was not one of those calls. Jeanette was at work when her cell phone vibrated in her pocket. She recognized the number as the school and excused herself from the room. What she heard from the counselor changed her life forever. Jeanette recounts the moment.

> *I answered the phone to hear the usual pleasantries one hears, when the caller knows they are interrupting. She asked if she had caught me at a bad time. I say to her that I am at work but I can talk (I had already informed her at the beginning of the year of my availability when it comes to my child).*
>
> *She proceeded to tell me that over the spring break something had happened to my child and she thought I should know. She placed my child on the phone and all she did was cry. I told her that I was on my way. I called my husband who was also at work and asked him to meet me at the school.*

We met at the school, and I shared with him the brief information that I had been given. As we walked to the doors of the school, I felt my heart beating against the walls of my chest. My hands and feet both began to sweat. We walked in to the office and they gave us directions to the counselor's office. She asked if I noticed anything different about my daughter. I knew what she meant right away but I didn't want to believe it. I told her that I had not noticed any changes in her.

My husband asked our daughter to come and sit on his lap. She laid her head on his broad shoulder and began to cry. He held her so gently and told her that she was not in trouble and that she could tell him anything. The air was dense as the counselor and her intern appeared to gawk at our family's pain. She then described to us a sexual assault.

As my heart sank to the pit of my stomach, I saw the anger and distress rise in my husband's eyes. I saw the look of embarrassment and shame on my daughter's face. The counselor continued to grill me about any changes in my child's behavior. I told her again that there had not been any. I checked my daughter out of school and took her to a local agency for service.

Jeanette continues to share her story as the tears flowing freely down her face, do not interfere with her vocals.

On the drive to the agency, I continued to reiterate to my child that it was not her fault and no matter how embarrassed she may feel; she is going to be asked to share this information again. In the counselor's office she had only given us a synopsis of what had occurred. I held back the tears as I tried to assure her that her father and I loved her. I let her know that her parents were going to do their best to make sure that the boy who had done this to her was held accountable. I tried to reassure her. I tried to give her all the love and support that I had inside of me. I tried to be there for her.

I know that I had checked out mentally in the counselor's office. It was as if, it was as if my mind would not allow me to comprehend the words that had just been spoken. How could this have happened? I asked myself this over and over again on the ride to the sexual assault agency. I looked over at my daughter. She laid her head against the window.

Jeanette's tears were now rolling in sync with the rain sliding off of the patio glass door. Jeanette continually tried to pin down the moment in which she made her error. Jeanette blamed herself for what had happened to her daughter. Jeanette felt as if she should have foreseen this event. She cried uncontrollably for ten minutes or so before continuing on.

You know my husband never wanted any of our children to spend the night at the homes of their friends. I always thought that he was being over protective and that you could not hinder them from the things that children do. I thought that knowing the parent was enough. There was no adult male

11

living in the home and I truly believed that there was not a cause for alarm. I was so wrong.

I know he blames me. He does not say it but he does. When he thinks about it, when he looks at her, I feel the contempt that he has for me and what I have allowed to happen to our first born. It won't happen again.

Jeanette's facial expression when she states, "it won't happen again" is stone. It is unmovable and unbreakable. She has made up in her mind that her children will never again become victim to the sexual deviances of another for as long as there was breath in her body. She was determined to protect her young at whatever cost. She could not bear the thought of not protecting this child again. As for the other children; she could not imagine them ever being able to handle such pain as her first born is now forced to deal with.

Counseling Session for Jeanette's Daughter

Jeanette immediately set a counseling appointment for her daughter to begin the healing process. She scheduled her appointment at the local agency in which she took her for the initial examination. The person who handled the walk-in for the crisis, created an environment in which Jeanette felt comfortable in bringing her child for continued care. Unfortunately, the continuum of care was not consistent.

Jeanette's daughter went to the initial counseling session. She felt comfortable in returning to see the young Caucasian female counselor. She felt that because of her youthfulness, there was an understanding of what she was going through and that this was going to be a good match. Her daughter had experience with other therapists (not related to the assault) in the past and was certain prior to meeting this one that it was not going to work. She was pleasantly surprised that this therapist was able to make a connection with her.

This feeling of contentment and satisfaction however was short lived. The next counseling appointment, she waited over 25 minutes for the therapist only to be told by someone else that she was unavailable. She was then sent to talk with someone whose expertise was not sexual assault and was just occupying the remainder of the time left in the session.

Jeanette's daughter felt put off and that her situation was not important to the therapist. She decided that she was not going to see her again.

She did not want to see another professional ever again. She had been reassured by the therapist that she would not feel the dissatisfaction that she had encountered with her previous therapists. However, what she now felt was one hundred times worse. Unlike with the previous professionals, she had actually shared with this one the truth of what was going on with her. She confided in her the shame; fear and guilt that was now walking side by side with her daily, only to be shut down by inconsistent service provision.

Her opportunity to prove to this teen that she was important and that this was not her fault had slipped through her fingers. The assumption in the provider's mind, that missing a teen's appointment would be harmless was an error that could not be undone. This nonchalant attitude toward the teen's time was a slap in the face to this young survivor.

The therapist did call to apologize. She tried to give an explanation. She began to speak of the crisis she had to handle, which only reiterated to Jeanette's daughter, that her crisis was not as important as others. For Jeanette's daughter, it said to her that what she was feeling needed to be dealt with by her alone and no one else. The therapist wanted a second chance, but it was not available to her. Sometimes you only get a single chance at getting it right.

Jeanette was determined to get help for her daughter. She asked around for an African American female counselor and/or therapist who were young and located in a fifty mile radius of her home. She was determined to get her daughter help even if it meant traveling to another city. She was fortunate in that what she was looking for did exist. Not only did she find a counselor, she was young, African American and one city over.

Of course, Jeanette's daughter wanted no parts in seeing another counselor. She tried desperately to prove to her mother that she was alright and that she no longer needed to talk to anyone. Through tears she pleaded with her mother to not make her see anyone else. She was embarrassed and did not want to relive her story with yet another stranger to be let down. Pulling at her mother's heart strings, she attempted to fight a losing battle. She would have won had Jeanette not experienced a sexual assault herself.

Jeanette attended the first session with the new therapist alongside her daughter. Her assessment of the session was this:

> *At first we could not find the place. It was at an undisclosed location unlike the one in our city. This made it more difficult as my daughter did not want to go. Once we found the place, she begged me not to make her go in. She said if I made her go she would not say anything to the therapist and then I would have wasted a trip. As much as I did not want to make her go, I did.*
>
> *I did not want her to grow up with this pain that would creep up in her life at the most inopportune time, and cause her to experience again the moment without relief, without an understanding of what was happening or how to deal with it. Having her deal with others treating her as if she was a freak for overreacting to a scene in a movie or a restraint in a child's game was more than I could handle.*

We arrived and completed the initial paperwork. The environment was soothing, similar to the environment at the local agency so it wasn't anything to get excited about. When the therapist came out to take her back, she would not go unless I went with her. The therapist agreed. It was not an agreement like whatever; it was more of what is best for you is what we will do.

We went to the counseling room; my daughter laid her head on my lap. She was refusing to talk as she said she would. The therapist was so gentle. She asked her if she wanted to be there. Of course my daughter said she did not. This did not dissuade the counselor. She continued to talk with her until she opened up. She assured her that if she did not want to share something that she did not have to. She also shared with her that they would work on her goals and what she wanted to get out of the sessions as she worked on healing.

As we left the building, my daughter hugged me and said thank you. The following sessions were just as productive and when my daughter felt things were moving too fast, she slowed down. She listened, she cared, she talked about things that were important to my daughter and allowed her to share with her the pain she was feeling. The therapist allowed her to be herself and to heal at her own pace. She was able to talk about being an African American dark skin teen and dealing with being sexualized. She was not superficial. She was the real deal. She was a God send.

Jeanette now overwhelmed by her emotions sits and sobs.

She explains that she is pleased with the counselor and her daughter's progress. She wanted to be able to do more for her daughter, but her daughter's assault was now forcing her to deal with her own stuff. I give Jeanette time to compose. Jeanette continues sobbing. "So many years have gone by" she states. She continues to sob. She is shaking her head and repeating herself over and over again.

Issues of the past that she thought were buried never to resurface are now staring her straight in the eyes. She tries desperately to wish her past her away, to imagine that it never happened. It isn't working for her. She tries to tell herself that she has healed, but the emotional response to her daughter's assault tells her otherwise. We end there for the day. Jeanette is tired and just wants to rest. She doesn't want to talk or be with others. She wipes her face and puts on a smile. She heads home to cook dinner for her family and to go on as if she is perfectly fine.

My life my world my beginning
The traps and tragedies are attempting to resurface
As I have moved on and placed those things behind me
They have attached themselves in ways unimaginable
Lessons of the past can't be learned if not shared
As I try to hide from the shame
I have myself to blame
I see the future of my offspring
Resonating so deeply within
Are the parents sins
The error of my ways
Are being played out today
As knowledge is given, the words are not received
Destined to repeat
Destined to mislead

Jeanette's Story

Jeanette returns about a week later. She is composed, freshly manicured and seemingly serene. She says that she took some time for self care before returning for her session. Jeanette begins with an apology for falling apart the last time that we met. She shares that she has been told that she needs to get over it and move on in order for healing to occur for her family.

I explain to her that apologies are not necessary and that she went through what she needed to go through in order to be here today. I also assured her, that whoever told her to get over it probably meant well. I explained, sometimes those who are close to us are at a loss for what to say. Patience is a gift that very few are able to give. She didn't have to just get over it. It was okay for her to take as much time as she needed to heal. I hand her the box of tissue as the water begins to well in her eyes. She says thank you with a pleasant smile and begins.

When I was ten years old, my parents divorced. The divorce was anything but cordial. To this day, over twenty years later they still are not able to hold a civil conversation. When my parents divorced, my father felt as if he had relinquished all of his parental duties. He no longer spent time with us, called us or participated in our upbringing.

My mom took a job, which was not necessarily on the up and up. She left us with people, who I am quite sure that if she and my father had been together we would have never met them. My younger siblings and I were dropped off at the home of the Shortness. The Shortness home was filthy. It was full of roaches, empty beer bottles, liquor bottles, cigarette ashes and dirty dishes. My mom was a very clean woman so this was a big shock to our system that people lived like this.

I remember not wanting to enter the home. The home had a stench. At the time, as child, I could not put my finger on it; but the stench was of sorrow, hurt and despair. My mom made us go in and assured us she would return when she was done working. My siblings and I huddled together in a corner. We held each other tight. All together we felt alone. We felt abandoned. We were offered food as the roaches crossed the counter and inhabited the bread sacks. We declined as our stomachs growled. As the oldest sibling, I made promises of bologna and cheese sandwiches when we returned home.

There were children at the Shortness home. A boy and a girl about the same age as my siblings, well the boy was a bit older. They seemed a bit odd. The boy wore glasses that were shaped like the bottom of coke bottles. He was not handsome at all. In fact had it not been for his oddness, one would be hard pressed to look at him over a second. His sister seemed a bit more outgoing and eager to gain the attention of anyone who would give it. My siblings and I were not impressed.

As the night moved on and the drinking and partying continued, my siblings and I grew tired. We were afraid to fall asleep. We were afraid that the roaches would crawl on us if we were to sleep. What seemed like an eternity had passed. One of the men in the Shortness family told us it was time for bed. We tried to assure them that we were fine right where we were, however; our powers of persuasion were not yet developed and we failed at our mission. We moved to the upstairs bedrooms.

Once a sleep, we were separated again. I was in a room that was filled with clothing all over the room. It appeared that the room had never been cleaned. As I lay there, wishing for my mom to return, one of the Shortness men appeared. He reeked of Colt 45, Kool cigarettes and a smell that I now know was crack cocaine. He laid his body on top of mine and told me to be quiet. I cried as he tried to kiss me. He began putting his hands in my pants and laying his penis against me. He was trying to penetrate. He fell asleep on top of me. I pushed him over and found my siblings.

When my mother arrived, she found us all together. I told her that I did not want to go back. My siblings and I all told her that we did not want to go back. A week later, we were back. We protested. We cried. We told her that we did not like it there and that we did not want to ever go back. She told us she had to work and with our father not doing his part she had no other options. She asked us if we wanted her to lose her job. Of course we did not want that.

We went into the home, once again clinging to each other. The events that had happened before were now happening again. I was in this filthy room lying on a pile of clothing contemplating what I would do if he returned. He returned, this time it was as if he had a determination like never before. He tried and tried to penetrate, but to no avail. He kissed and rubbed on me and then he was interrupted by another one of the Shortness trying to assure me that everything would be okay.

We never went back after that night. I never spoke a word to my mother about the incident. I don't know to this day if the Shortness who interrupted told her about the incident. If he did, she never said anything to me about it. She never inquired or sent me for help. I was never the same after that.

I don't know what my mother's reaction would have been had I told her. I still have moments today when I want to tell her. I don't. I keep quiet. I am afraid she will not believe me. I am afraid that she will blame me. I am afraid that she knows and did nothing to save me.

Jeanette's feelings are very common among those who have suffered an assault. Many go through life never telling a soul about the assault in their lives. She thought this incident had been integrated as just another part of her life. She believed that she had survived and moved on. Now, she feels haunted by her past. Determined to move on with her life and assist her daughter through the recovery process, she continues on with her story.

I was almost thirteen. I was living in an apartment with my mother close to a college campus. It was a nice place where our neighbors changed often. I often walked a few miles or rode the bus to friend's home for entertainment. In the spring, a family moved into the complex.

The family consisted of a girl my age and an Aunt (the guardian of the girl). We didn't have much in common other than our age. She barely attended school and was a couple of grades behind me. Shortly thereafter, her brother moved into the apartment with them. Her brother who was freshly released from prison at the age of 22 was flirting with me. I was not remotely, interested in him. His breath smelled of cheap cigar smoke and his metal mouth smile was less than desirable. He was not even close to being considered attractive to me. Every opportunity that arose, he made advances toward me. I always thought it was harmless.

One day I made a foolish decision. I agreed to cut school with his sister. We hung out at her apartment. The whole time we were there, she constantly tried to leave me alone with her brother. Her Aunt kept telling me that he was so fond of me. I left there with no harm to me.

A few days later, she and I fell out. She came to my apartment yelling and screaming obscenities. She and her Aunt were both telling my mother that I had intercourse with this guy. What made this lie so devastating to my relationship with my mother was the mere fact that it was being told by an adult. Most adults have an unspoken rule; an adult would

23

not lie on a child so always believe the adult. This unspoken rule was one of many nails in the coffin of our relationship.

A young immature mind such as mine at the time thinks; if you are going to be accused of something and suffer consequences, at least let it be true. That was when I decided that if I were going to have sex it would be on my terms. No one would decide for me, no one would force me I would be in control of my own sexual self. At least that's what I thought, life taught me otherwise.

Most of my teen years, I would find myself in unhealthy relationships. I would be coerced and forced into having sex by those who pretended to love me. They said it would make a woman out of me. For a while, I never thought I would make it to adulthood.

Jeanette is indicating that the assault of her daughter has interrupted her ability to suppress her own assaults. Jeanette has been victimized on more than one occasion and it has gone unnoticed by those who are closest to her. Her teen and childhood years have been riddled with those who took advantage of a young woman who was vulnerable. She was not protected. The needs of her and her siblings were placed second to the basic needs of life.

The family needed money in order to provide a roof over their heads, as well as food and clothing. If the basic needs are not met, everything else waits. This is clearly reflected in Jeanette's life. The love and care that the she and her siblings needed was given in the form of food and shelter. Jeanette's mother was a proud woman who worked tirelessly to avoid being seen as lazy and reliant on the government for assistance.

Her experience with racism growing up in the 50's and 60's, unequivocally shaped her parenting. Jeanette recollects how her mother spoke frequently of how important it was to not have to ask Whites for anything. Without extended support, Jeanette's mom was present for her family in the only way she knew how.

Jeanette is providing for her family to the best of her ability. She has to learn from lessons that she did not receive. Jeanette is parenting out of a wounded past. The failure of proper intervention in her life has left her weary. The distrust of adults and those in authority over her has caused her to be closed off to healing for herself.

Emotional barriers that were created in her past directly impact the way in which she can be given services. It is paramount to explore those barriers before deciding on the goals of service. The best laid plan is not a plan at all if the survivor cannot comprehend it. The underlying issues of pain and abuse must be concentrated on in order to properly address the issue that brought them to our door today. A willingness to attend to past hurt and acknowledge the influence it has on a survivors life today, creates an atmosphere of trust.

Perceptions of CPS

A known barrier to individuals seeking help for domestic and sexual violence is a fear of involvement by child protective services (CPS). Individuals may go a lifetime without ever disclosing, for fear of having their children removed by this system. There are negative perceptions and experiences that support this fear. Many families have had CPS as an uninvited part of their lives. This may occur at a time when a family is seeking services.

An advocate, who is trying to do the right thing for the survivor, makes a report. The system does not respond in a way in which the client can see as positive. How do we as service providers, go forth with a clear conscience knowing that we may share in the responsibility for the stress and feeling of hopelessness that a person expresses simply from having contact with CPS?

We can gain an understanding of the reporting laws. Service providers, who are so eager to protect their license, forget who it is they are supposed to be responsible for. Services are not rendered based on self-determination, but on policy and procedure. I am an advocate for everyone gaining an understanding of policy and procedure. Gaining an understanding of policy and procedure will allow for a service provider to recognize the power that they have; the power of discretion.

While some CPS workers would love for you to bombard them with anything and everything you think may constitute child abuse, it is a campaign that is detrimental to the well-being of families. Child Protective Services has worked hard to reinvent the way the public views them. As an advocate, you are charged with assuring the survivor sees the agency on its face value and not through the lenses of an overzealous worker.

There are specific guidelines that are to be followed before making a report and they vary state to state. Children should be protected however, being a survivor of abuse does not make one unfit. Many service providers do not understand the concept of discretion, yet it is a concept that is exercised regularly by some CPS workers. Thus, you have the varied and inconsistent response to allegations when a report is made due to a survivor's need for services.

Making a report to CPS when a child is not in danger is nothing more than re-victimization of the survivor. A survivor who is re-victimized will have a setback in their journey towards recovery. Depending on the outcome of the investigation, the survivor may never be able to integrate the incident as a trauma experienced in their life. The relationship between the survivor and the service provider in many cases is strained as the trust has been betrayed. The survivor is no longer continuing with sessions based on a voluntary relationship in which they initiated, but by a mandate from CPS.

The survivor has been completely stripped of their power and is now forced to share the intimate details of their assault with someone whom they no longer see as an ally. The survivor is now choosing her words with care as to not self-incriminate any further, for fear of the effect it may have on her family. She is no longer on the path toward healing, but on the path of self-preservation and the protection of her family.

I would never advocate for a service provider to place their license in harm's way. I am advocating for the service provider to understand what needs to be reported and what does not. Once child protective services enter your life, it is a process to remove them. A report that is made cannot be undone. A family betrayed by the service provider they chose to help them will only distance themselves from systems.

Instead of seeking help for those things in which they cannot handle alone they will try desperately to work it out themselves. They cannot afford to have their family business made public and scrutinized with the risk of losing their family. A damaged relationship between the survivor and the service provider is difficult to repair. In many cases you only receive one chance to assist.

Before allowing a survivor to disclose information that may be to their detriment, it is your responsibility to inform the survivor of what you feel obligated to report. If you recognize that you are a person who regardless of the circumstance will not utilize discretion, it is your obligation to share this information. An advocate is responsible for being transparent during service provision.

Make sure that the survivor is clear. It is not adequate to do this only at intake or the initial session. Most survivors are in a state of crisis and are only going through the motions. It is your obligation to make sure a survivor is clear on what it is you deem necessary to report. A client has the right to receive this message from you in intervals. One of the most heart-wrenching conversations I have ever had with a survivor involved the removal of her children after she sought shelter for domestic violence. Jeanette shares her experience with CPS.

Deceiver
I was a believer
Do unto others as you'd want them to do unto you
Oh you better pray that those words aren't true
Deceived
You deceived me said you needed me
As you used and abused me
Deceit
Never have I encountered so much deceitfulness
The lies and trail of traps you set for hopelessness
Deceiver
I am not a believer
Defrauded for the very last time
Established my boundaries keep your dime
Deceived
Keep your deceit let me be
Leave me be
Stay the hell away from me
Your day is coming

The African American counselor who I thought was a God send ended up being a wolf in sheep's clothing. I called one day. This particular day, I was frantic. I had received a call that my daughter had acted out sexually towards another child. She assured me that everything would be alright. I felt relieved.

Two days later she called me and said she was obligated to make a CPS report. I was devastated. Within an hour of telling me this, CPS called and threatened to remove my children. They told me that I had to file a police report against my own child or they would do it and seek to remove my children. It was a nightmare. Here I was sitting on my front porch. My children were in the fenced in backyard playing freely while I wrestled with what was to come. Of course I had to make the police report. I could not let my children be taken away from me.

I continued taking my daughter to see the counselor long enough to get CPS off my back. I shared with my daughter the importance of choosing her words and the implications they may have on the household.

It was stupid of me to call the therapist. My family had warned me of trusting systems. They said, "They will tell you anything to get the information they want". I thought this was different. I really believed she would help us.

To better assist clients who are engaged with CPS, the service provider must have a working relationship with the entity. Collaborating with an agency such as CPS allows for each agency to: meet the needs of the client, understand the goals of each agency, and accomplish those goals without undermining each other or sacrificing the client and their family. Collaboration allows for cross-training opportunities as well as networking. In order for the collaboration to work for our clients, we must be truthful with them every step of the way. Transparency is essential. Full disclosure and the sharing of expectations will allow for trust to be built.

Jeanette was provided services without regard to her culture. She believed being an African American; the service provider would understand her. She believed the service provider was working from the same cultural perspective as she. Unfortunately for Jeanette, this was not the case. Diversity affects the way in which we experience our culture. Her daughter's therapist did not share the same life experiences as Jeanette and her family. In fact, while Jeanette had grown up in poverty, her daughter's therapist had grown up upper middle class with educated parents who shielded her from racism to the best of their ability.

Their truths and realities were not the same. Both the therapist and Jeanette were working from their own experience and both had valid perspectives. However, it was not for Jeanette to learn the background of the therapist. It was the therapist who needed to do the work to find out how best to service this family. Jeanette's reality was that systems were untrustworthy. The therapist could have simply asked Jeanette what her feelings were regarding seeking services.

It is not uncommon for many people of color to have a distrust of systems. This distrust predates the existence of domestic and sexual assault services. There is a legacy of unfair treatment of people of color by systems. The lessons that are learned by those who have been let down by various systems is passed down through the generations. As we gain an understanding of the culture of our clients, we will be in a position to provide appropriate services and resources while differentiating ourselves from other systems.

The therapist had knowledge of sexual violence and self-esteem issues of girls of color. This information was necessary in gaining the trust of the family but was not enough to maintain it. When working with survivors of color, we are working with the family and not just the survivor. If the therapist had understood this dynamic, the healing of the daughter may not have been interrupted. The daughter was removed from this therapist's care for fear that the actions of the therapist would cause further harm to the family unit.

Why Am I Engaged In This Work

There are many fields of work that require one to practice "self-examination" to analyze if the duties are more than they can handle. Sexual and Domestic Violence work are no exception. Many come to this field of work for various reasons. Some come with the intention of helping others. Some come with the desire to save the world. Others come to this line of work due to preconceived notions about the type of people who are doing the work. There are many who are here solely on the fact that they were looking for employment and an opening became available.

I have not stepped foot in an agency where a survivor was not employed in some capacity; as many survivors are drawn to this work out of their own victimization. This can be very positive in relating to the person in front of you. It can also be an issue if you are seeing yourself instead of the client. Quite a few survivors may not disclose their survivorship (nor should they be required). While there is no <u>one</u> reason that you may come by this work, there are some things to consider when deciding if this is the line of work for you.

One should always take into consideration before working in any field, the way in which it fits with their belief system. Working with survivors requires individuals who are capable of setting aside their own bias to assist the survivor on their journey of healing. It requires that if you are a survivor, you are dealing with the survivorship of the person meeting with you, not your own. If you recognize that you are not comfortable in working with people from backgrounds that do not resemble your own, you may want to consider the following options.

The first option I would recommend is to do some self-work. Seek out opportunities that will allow you to explore the root of your discomfort. Anti-bias as well as anti-racism workshops can be extremely beneficial. Activities that you seek out for yourself will be more meaningful than those that are mandated by an employer. Activities may include volunteering and attending multicultural events.

The second option will be to explore a new career path. While this work may provide a means of supporting you, if you are not willing to learn on an ongoing basis ways in which to improve your service provision, this is not the field for you and you may in fact be causing harm. A desire to work with those who you view as less fortunate is not enough to justify a position along their journey. Being a humanitarian while displaying no empathy is callous. A lack of empathy sabotages all of your efforts to make a positive difference in a survivor's life.

A survivor's lifestyle may not coincide with what you deem to be reasonable (something that is extremely important when counseling others whose cultural beliefs vary from your own), and you must be willing to focus on the task at hand not deviating to changing aspects of the survivor. A conviction that your culture is superior to those who you serve will produce peril. A survivor will share limited information with you and it will be superficial. The fruit of your work will be non-existent.

While providing supportive counseling, many of the

stories that we will listen to, may not have anything to do with the assault itself, but is an important aspect in the life of the person. Everything that is mentioned does not need to be addressed. However, it is essential to acknowledge what has been said. Many times a person wants only to be heard. We will go further with this discussion later on.

Personal healing of an advocate should not take place during sessions in which they are the advocator. Some advocates are survivors themselves who come to assist those who were hurt in the way in which they once were. Some have not quite healed from that hurt and casualties are the result. A survivor's story may bring about a feeling of re-victimization for an advocate that has not dealt with his/her own issues. In the event that this occurs, an advocate needs to seek assistance from her supervisor. If this has happened in the past, review the outcome, what could be done differently and seek counseling for yourself.

While disclosure of one's own survivorship can be beneficial in building a rapport with the client, it is not to be done without purpose. Disclosure with a survivor is very delicate. If not done properly, the session may turn into you being cared for by the person whom initially sought you for service. While this is certainly not the intention of the provider, it causes great harm to the client.

Each survivor responds differently to what may appear to be the same set of circumstances. Each aspect of a person makes those similar circumstances distinctive. In essence, what may have helped you heal may not help the survivor.

When I first came to this line of work, I thought that I would be able to "save" each and every family in which I came in contact with from the clutches of the cycle of violence. Yes, I was very naive. I soon learned that I was not to be the savior.

Thanks to the many survivors who were willing to speak candidly with me, I learned that they were not looking for someone to save them. Coming to the program, the survivor was looking for someone to affirm that they were not crazy. They were searching for that person who could name what had been occurring in their life. They were seeking assistance as they transitioned.

Working with survivors is very demanding. This work has to be its own reward. We are in place to provide a service that is matchless to all others. Free of charge we will not require a survivor to partake in any of the services that we may offer if she has not identified it as a need. We may never see the immediate fruits of our labor.

This is not the field to be in if you need to have a client tell you that have made a life altering change in their lives. Not to say that survivors are not thankful for the support. This is to say that it is because of them that we do the work. We need to acknowledge the privilege that we have been afforded by them allowing us into the most intimate part of their life. Therefore, it would be wise of us to move with humility as we work with survivors.

Empathy and Compassion

The capacity to empathize with a person is a proficiency that is taken for granted. For the people we are employed to journey alongside of, empathy is a consideration that is of priority. Social service type work usually requires that a person has a degree in social work or related field. If they don't have a degree they are typically required to have an equivalent amount of experience. The educational or work related experience is the first criterion that has to be met for employment. Empathy skills are not listed amongst the requirements. To empathize with a person, you need only allow yourself to understand where he/she may be coming from. It is not pity; it is not sympathy, but an expression of identifying with a feeling of another.

How many times have we witnessed a person in a position to make a difference, turn a person a way? When the person was turned away, the service provider justified the actions by utilizing language that was belittling toward the individual. Judgmental and feeling oneself as superior to the person who you are charged with providing a service to, tends to create an environment of hostility and distrust.

The language that we use to define the service that we provide guides the way in which we work. Language that is patronizing and demeaning set the ground work for services to be given in the same manner. The language that we use when applying for grants, reaching the community, and speaking with those who we intend to service needs to be consistent. If we are using different language in those areas we need to re-evaluate the work we are doing. Taking an inventory of why we have chosen this particular work and our intended target recipients will refocus us. If we have chosen a particular group to service, is the need real or perceived? Have we done our work to assure that we are meeting the people where they are? Are we positioning ourselves to be saviors and benevolent to those who we have deemed to be lowly and beneath us?

Non-profit agencies are usually created with the intention of providing services to those who are in need. An issue is identified and products and services are created around that need. Data from research and evaluations are the drivers of the service. However, the research and evaluation process rarely takes into account culture. Without taking into account culture, we are seen as carrying an attitude that diminishes that positive attributes of a people.

Often it is said by agencies that our focus is not culture, it is education, sexual violence, domestic violence, poverty, and the list goes on. Reality check; none of the above occurs in the absence of culture. Denying the existence of culture does not make it invisible. A denial that culture needs to be a consideration in the way we provide services does not diminish its truth.

The propensity to show empathy for our clientele is a requirement. Compassion; consideration and respect for our clientele are also a requirement. Lack of empathy and compassion make for services that are given for the sake of giving services. Needs are not being met without incorporating culture and empathy in a significant manner.

An employee would be hard-pressed to display coldness and self-righteousness in an environment where an individual is given respect. An agency that operates with empathy as a core requirement for service provision will see growth beyond measure.

Sexual Violence

The African American woman has been stigmatized in American society. She has and continues to be depicted as promiscuous and as having an insatiable sexual appetite. Daily you can find images that reflect her as being ignorant and immoral. She's seen as an addict, welfare recipient, video girl, pole dancer and someone who will do anything for a dollar. This depiction of her leaves her viewed as incapable of being raped. This alleged inability to be raped, prevents many women from coming forward. They are much more likely to see themselves as deserving of their assault.

At times this myth is further perpetuated in the communities in which they reside. Women of color are told they are strong and impenetrable. Women of color are told to be the glue that holds the family together. They are told to suffer in silence so as not to bring undue attention to their male counterpart.

Historically, any involvement with systems has been deemed detrimental to the man of color. The woman of color has had to be mother and father in her home. There are instances in which her own safety and well-being has been placed last to the wholeness of the family unit. She dare not take a place of priority in her life; it is seen as selfishness.

With all of the pressure from family and community,

women of color at times internalize the myths. They find themselves feeling unworthy of love. They find themselves evaluating their worthiness by the number of men who want to sleep with them. Each day, the images of beauty do not reflect who women of color are. They do not reflect the dynamics of their family accurately and again she finds herself having to protect, to the best of her ability, the image of her family. What is the cost of this to the woman?

Women of color often find themselves at service providing agencies for various reasons. One reason is that others (outside of the community and family unit) have intervened. This intervention could be a 911 call, a CPS call, or even a referral from another agency. This well intended intervention may not work. While all evidence may support that an assault has taken place, she may refuse to cooperate in an effort to protect her family.

There is a burden that many women of color carry that cannot be fully explained to someone who has not had to walk in those shoes. The shame and guilt of an assault is compounded by the expectation of strength beyond reason. This silence is then passed on to their daughters for generations. Many women of color are hard pressed to come forward for fear of communal isolation. Instead of coming forward and giving the authorities' information on her assault, the woman may deny an incident has occurred. This mythical protection has been given strength by the many prosecutors who won't go forward with charges without a victim's testimony or substantial physical evidence. The lack of charges does damage in two very clear ways.

First it allows for the woman to be further victimized by not protecting her. Even though she did not seek a remedy for the assault, someone or some entity intervened. Without the backing of prosecution, this intervention is at a standstill. The prosecutions unwillingness to move forward also allows for the community at large to further doubt that an assault has taken place. Unfortunately for women of color, if the prosecution says there is not enough evidence to proceed, she is abandoned by her community.

Secondly, the lack of charges gives the assailant a sense of invincibility. Not going forward with charges, the assailant becomes someone who is not to be reckoned with. She was told no one would believe her and/or do anything to help her. This lack of moving on with charges lends credibility to what she has been told by her abuser.

The many brave women who have come forward have been met with disbelief and a seemingly unyielding campaign to destroy her. The list of stories that have garnered national attention, all share one common thread; she has to be proven credible before the assault charges are taken seriously. If she is found to have any blemish in her past, then the results have typically not been favorable. Under these conditions, what would propel women to continue coming forward?

Women of color who are sexually victimized often operate out of crisis. Operating out of crisis means they are no longer functioning in a state of being that is normal for them. A person who is operating out of crisis may have a difficult time making sound decisions. For many survivors, operating in crisis mode is not recognized. This goes unrecognized for many reasons.

One reason this may go unrecognized is the number of women in the community who are also operating in crisis. A person would find it difficult to assist a person in need of help when they are in need themselves. Another cause is the lack of, or perceived lack of available assistance. If a person doesn't believe that assistance is available to them, the likelihood of them seeking it is slim.

There is yet another explanation the operating out of crisis may go unrecognized. It is the stigma of the "angry black woman". Many women of color, who boldly attempt to use their voice, are often met with opposition. They are viewed as angry, hostile and difficult to work with. They are often put off and left to figure it out on their own. The very service providers that are in position to assist, don't out of an unsubstantiated fear. They are afraid of what this angry black woman might say or do to them.

The stereotyping of women of color, not only destroys their working relationship, but it hinders the ability of other systems to help her. The ignorance and bias does not allow them to advocate appropriately for the survivor. The fear overshadows any rational thought process. Each decision that is needed to effectively work on behalf of the survivor is done with apprehension.

Here is an illustration for you: A woman comes in to your agency seeking sexual violence services. As you go through the questionnaire with her, she raises her voice and wants to know why you need so much information. As the service provider, do you shut down and refuse to work with her as you don't have to be treated like that? Do you listen to her and try to find out what she dislikes about the line of questions? What do you base your response to her on? Does your response to her vary depending on her culture? Should it?

If we stop and recognize the nature of the work we do, it will be obvious to us that this person may be operating out of crisis. Our goal is to guide her out of her crisis to what is normal to her. A rising of a voice is not indicative of someone who is going to be difficult to work with or of someone who is angry. A rising of the voice can be a signal that someone is unclear of the process and may have a fear of the unknown.

It is critical to avoid assumption. It is imperative that one take the time to ask and seek clarification from the survivor. Asking and seeking clarification only lends to the credibility of the service provider and the agency. It breaks down barriers and can assist in myth debunking and elimination of stereotypes held by both the helper and the help seeker. Jeanette shares why she herself never sought help.

> *I always thought about talking to someone about what had happened to me. In high school, the teachers and counselors would say you could talk to them about anything. Well one day I decided to test the waters. I tried talking to my guidance counselor a little bit about my home life. When I saw the look on the counselors face, I knew it was not a good idea to share any other information. The counselor looked as if she couldn't believe what she was hearing.*
>
> *I often listened to the women around the neighborhood talk about being violated. It was never pleasant, yet it gave me direction on how to handle what was going on with me. Their stories made it clear to me what course of action to take. The thought of going to a hospital and being further violated scared me. They would say things like, the doctors were poking and prodding like they didn't know I was just raped. The officer was asking me all these questions and wouldn't let me get dressed. They would ask for his name like they were going to do something and then tell me that it was up to the*

> *prosecutor. All of these people looking at me. Their eyes were saying that something was extremely wrong with me. Not a single person looked like me or could relate to where I was from. After hearing all those things, I knew I could not say anything to anyone. Who wants to go through that?*

Jeanette's experience provides us with a clue as to how our clients formulate their opinions on service provision. The perceptions of those who have utilized the services shape the way in which others determine how and when to use them. It is just a glimpse into the way information (factual or not) is disseminated in communities of color.

We can combat this information by assuring the information in communities is up-to-date. When Jeanette was contemplating seeking services, there were no Nurse Examiner programs. Sexual Assault programs were relatively new. Marital rape was not illegal in all 50 states. Educators in the field of Domestic and Sexual violence were not being invited into schools. Media Campaigns that focused on intimate partner violence were unheard of.

The ability therefore, to make an informed decision if you found yourself victimized was very limited. With the availability of sexual assault and domestic violence agencies today, a new dynamic has been created where a person has options. Knowledge of these options among community members can aid a woman in making an informed decision regarding their care.

Many women of color express a sense of conservativeness when it comes to reproductive health. The majority of women of color I have spoken with express being pro-life and pro-family. This belief is contrary to how women of color are depicted and contrary to the way in which reproductive as well as sexual and domestic violence agencies appear to be. The appearance in the community of agencies that have roots in the feminist movement, is when it comes to sexuality, anything goes. With this belief floating through the community, many women of color try to steer the younger women of color away.

The fear of having someone teaching/telling your daughter that she has the right to have sex (even though she is not of age) is contrary to the belief system of many families. Many reproductive clinics will not share a teen's information with the custodial parent, yet asking for insurance information. However, this does not create an environment of trust. It certainly begins the relationship without common ground.

Confidentiality is meant to protect a person. It is meant to allow for a person to speak freely and not have the conversation go anywhere. Confidentiality can bring peace of mind to a woman seeking protection from abuse. Yet when it comes to a teen and sexuality, confidentiality is not something that some parents of color are comfortable with.

The parents that I have spoken to have expressed sorrow in learning that what they deemed to be harmful, was not deemed harmful by the service provider. In fact, the service providers they worked with did not have an issue with 13 and 14 year old teens engaging in sexual activity. This was regardless if they had reached the age of consent (also varies state to state). Here is what happened with Jeanette's daughter.

I went to a therapist and she said I could trust her
Now my mama said that if a person doesn't have
your best interest at heart, don't trust them
So she told me about confidentiality and
that I could tell her anything

Said she'd only tell if I were hurting
myself or someone else
She said I could trust her
So I wanted some help so I took the steps
I chanced it all and shared it
Promiscuity and humiliation
Not once did she break confidentiality
I told her of sex at school with a senior
I told her how I compromised myself
Being bullied and degraded
Not once did she break confidentiality
I told her that I felt alone and tired
and didn't want to live no more
I told her that I couldn't control myself
I told her of my anger and lack of patience
I told her how I wanted to explode
Not once did she break my confidentiality
I told her I was thirteen
I told her that he was seventeen
I told her of being unprotected
She said I could do what I wanted
And my mom had to accept it
I failed classes, spiraled deeper
And she kept it to herself
What about what's best for me
She replied
Confidentiality

I felt betrayed on many levels by all the therapist and counselors that my daughter shared with. My daughter was making decisions that could impact not only her life, but our family's as well. One day my daughter and I were lying across the bed watching a movie when she disclosed to me that she had been having sex. Not only had she been having sex, but before she decided to, she told her counselor. Her counselor encouraged her and told her that she was in charge of her own sexuality and that it was important for her to take ownership. After she had sex, she also shared it with her counselor who promised her that she would not tell me.

I told the counselor prior to her meeting with my daughter, our stance on premarital sex. She told me that she understood. Clearly, that was a lie. Clearly, she could care less about the best interest of my child. The counselor trusted a 13 year old to be responsible. So for months, my child was having unprotected sex in places that were not good.

The whole time the counselor knew. The counselor knew and said nothing to me. The counselor did not care about her safety. All she cared about was her "so-called" confidentiality. Now that the relationship with the counselor is over, I am left to pick up the pieces. I took my daughter to the doctor and the doctor said she would not disclose without my daughters permission!

I have all the responsibility of caring for this child, yet the law says I don't have a say so? I promise that I will never, ever go to another agency. We will work through whatever issues come our way by ourselves. The worst part about this is that they made it right for her to disobey. Sex before marriage is something that is against our religious beliefs. Premarital sex, especially as a teen gives you baggage. One day my

*daughter will not be with this boy and it is I who
will have to deal with her broken heart. It is I who
will have to try and prevent her from carrying that
baggage on to the next relationship. I am telling all
my friends about this experience so they don't make
the same mistake that I made.*

I arise early each day
Eagerly awaiting the soothing sensation
Of the gentle warmth of the morning sun
I am instead greeted by the pitter patter
Of small feet the chatter of the small voices of those who
Came through my womb far too soon
As the sun inches its way through the panels of the blinds
I miss it as the soap and water cleanse my outer shell
I adorn myself with the body butter that has a hint of
perfume I place the color of red along the frame of my face
Energized and vitalized I await the challenges of the day
The challenges are too numerous to wrap
my mind around but I must persist
Persistence isn't far enough to sustain me through
the turmoil of mothering, wifeyness, so I must
pray for strength courage and guidance
My face radiates beauty to all whom
I meet as I give all that I have
Leaving my vessel almost depleted
I add some red to my lick-able lips to conceal the sting
of the words that wish to concede, admitting defeat
Am I transparent can you see the pain of years of self-
doubt years of trying to be everything to everyone?
Can you see me do you notice that my

graceful walk is no more than tip-toeing on
eggshells while balancing a loaded gun
The expectations of perfection
The unconditional love of you
The desire to have the ability to make the tough decisions
The desire for you to see my Red as Blue

Jeanette feels alone. She feels helpless and undermined by the very agencies she entrusted to assist in bringing healing to her family. She has also decided to share this information with others in her sphere of influence. We all have credibility within our sphere. What is the likelihood that those in Jeanette's sphere will seek help at a sexual assault agency?

Domestic Violence

Domestic violence as well as sexual violence does not discriminate. It does not matter where you live, where you grew up, how much money you have or don't have; domestic violence as well as sexual violence can find its way into your life. Those who have achieved an education are not exempt. For women of color, the impact of racism and internalized oppression on their community creates an environment where domestic violence devastates.

In spite of all the PSA's and literature about domestic violence, it continues to be pervasive in the community. Domestic violence goes unrecognized when there is no evidence of physical battering. It is easily ignored when the definition of abuse does not include isolation, withholding of money, and verbal abuse. It is dismissed when viewed as a tool used to dismantle families. It can be rejected when observed as a pawn in custody and divorce.

With issues that affect the whole community such as racial profiling and loss of jobs, the issue of domestic violence is left largely unaddressed. It is seen as a woman's issue and not something that affects the whole community. Silence and blame become the response to the violence she is suffering. The woman is again left to feel as if she is guilty for what is happening to her.

He said come here beautiful
Let me look at you close
The curves are calling me
Your walk is pulling me
Come here beautiful

He said let me call you sometime
The sound of your voice and the
Inflection in your speech
I want to be the one you see
Come here beautiful
He said let me hold your hand
The softness of your skin
I want it to intertwine with mine
You're so beautiful…come
And I went…
He said come hear ugly
Let me look at you close
The awkward shape of you turns me off
Your gallop is sickening to me
Get over here ugly
He said when I call you better answer
Don't let your phone ring twice
The squeal in your voice and that
Stupid ass accent makes me sicker
Come here ugly
He said give your hand
Who's been touching your skin?
I can smell him
You cheating whore
You so f@!% ugly
Come here ugly
And I went

Those who choose to abuse do not say to their victim, they are going to make their lives hell. They do not share that they will slowly tear them down and belittle them constantly. An abuser doesn't say they will isolate you from your family and friends. An abuser does not share, that the only point of view in the relationship that is of importance is his/hers.

Unfortunately, the responsibility to end the abuse is placed at the feet of the victim. Rarely do you find that the batterer is held accountable. The question is never why does he abuse? The question is always why does she stay, or why doesn't she leave?

There are numerous reasons as to why women find themselves unable to get out of these dangerous relationships. For all women, there are many factors. Here are a few reasons that are common among women of color.

One factor is children. Children are often used as leverage in keeping a woman in a relationship. A woman may be told that she is going to lose her children if she leaves. She might have not been given the opportunity to bond with her children. She may also be dealing with feelings of guilt. She may view herself as being responsible for the demise of the family unit.

For a woman of color, the shame faced when raising children alone may not be what she is willing to accept. Realizing that children of color are often raised without both parents in the home can be a consideration in deciding whether or not to leave the home. Time after time, women of color are told that many problems in the community are a result of fatherless children. However, it isn't communicated enough, the damage that may arise from children who are reared in homes where there is violence.

Another factor that may contribute to keeping a woman in an abusive relationship is homelessness. The inability to make purchases without producing a receipt is a reality for many women. Many women who are in abusive relationships are also financially abused. Not being allowed to work or having to turn over ones check leaves a person in a financial bind. Debt may have also been accumulated in the victim's name. Employers as well as landlords conducting credit checks are seen as barriers.

Yet another important factor that may keep a woman in an abusive relationship is safety. It is a known fact for those who work with survivors, the most dangerous time for a woman in the relationship is when she decides to end it. This time period is dangerous to a woman as she has taken some control away from the batterer. What has become known is batterers exert as much power over a woman that he feels is necessary to control her. For some women, this means that leaving the relationship can end in her death.

All of the above factors are compounded for the woman of color when you add on the layer of community stigmas. People continue to lock their doors when a person of color crosses the street. Many people will not let the sun fall down on them if they are in a neighborhood that is predominately people of color. In service provision, the ignoring of you as an individual member of your culture can be to say the least, a challenge.

The reality that many women of color face is this; they represent their entire community in every move they make. This seldom spoken truth has been reiterated to women of color in employment, housing and education. If a crime happens in a community of color, the community is seen as crime ridden. When a crime is committed in a neighborhood that is not of color, it is seen as an unfortunate incident. If a child of color performs badly in school, it is seen as a community issue, not of the individual family or child. If an employer hires a person of color who doesn't meet expectations, the employer may feel justified in not hiring other people of color.

The onus of reflecting positively on the community is on her shoulders. If she calls the police, if she tells someone outside of the community what is happening to her, she is viewed as a traitor. Women don't choose abuse; they choose to be as safe as possible.

Jeanette did not recognize the abusive relationships that she found herself in as domestic violence. Intimate partner violence was not a topic of discussion in the high schools. She was a teen. As a teen she believed that abuse happened to those who deserved it.

When I was in high school, I had a friend who was on the track team. She was dating a guy on the football team. They had been dating for a while and he yelled at her constantly. This day was like any other, he was arguing with her. What was unusual was she was arguing back. The next thing I knew, there was a large crowd surrounding them. He grabbed her by the throat and put her face in the locker. No one intervened. Not even the teachers who witnessed the incident. All I could think was why didn't she just shut up.

A few weeks later, I was in a similar situation. I was walking home from school and I saw some friends. We were talking and laughing when my boyfriend told me to come here. I didn't go because I was talking to my friends and he was being rude. He came over and grabbed me. He began yelling and saying didn't I hear him tell me to come here. I knew he was going to hit me. At that moment, one of my male friends drove up and intervened. I felt that if he would have hit me, I would have deserved it. I felt like I provoked him. I knew what he was capable of. We had fought before. He had forced himself on me several times. He would apologize afterward and then tell me that he knew I liked it.

I attempted to avoid him. He would call my house to curse me out. He would call several times a night and then say he was coming over. One night he stood on my porch calling me names and telling me I had to come out of the house at some point. I was scared. He was right. I had to face him at some point.

Fortunately for me, he was arrested later that night on drug charges. However, he continued to harass me through his family. His mother called and told me that he had bought me an engagement ring. His sister was watching me at school to see who I was talking to. I just needed to get away. At the end of the year my school was closed due to budget cuts. I was transferred to a school in another district. I have not heard from him or his family since.

Jeanette and her friend both were victims. They were involved intimately with their abusers. They were both afraid. Without intervention, her friend was left alone. She was in a public place, being abused with many witnesses including an adult who chose not to intervene. What message did they internalize about being abused?

The lessons that are learned about intimate partner

violence are often taught without words. We condone the violence when we witness it and do nothing to stop it. We silence the victim when we turn our heads. We isolate them when we watch without action. The message we send is clear. There is no help for you. You are powerless. He is powerful.

> **Today I smiled**
> **I smiled as I considered the future**
> **I considered the aspects of my future and**
> **the various fruits that it will bring**
> **The fruits are what I receive from the work I have done**
> **Today I laughed**
> **I laughed when I contemplated the things that will be**
> **I contemplated the life that I will live**
> **The life I will live and the hope of tomorrow**
> **Today I shed a tear**
> **I shed a tear for all the things that I cannot change**
> **I cannot change anyone but myself**
> **Self-reflection enlightenment as I move on**
> **Today I spoke up**
> **I spoke up for the things that I have witnessed**
> **I have witnessed many things and turned a blind eye**
> **My eyes are open and I can see**
> **Today I am whole**
> **I am whole as I know who I am**
> **I am who He says I am no one can differ**
> **They cannot differ from the words of my creator**

As a service provider, you are in a position to be a change agent. You can give information that may literally change the course of a person's life. We want to allow room for women to see that they do have power in their relationships. While the abuser is responsible for his behavior, she can be empowered to live abuse free. This can be achieved by being firm in setting and maintaining our boundaries.

An abuser may not tell you up front that he's going to be abusive, but he does cross boundaries early on. We must encourage limits on what is allowable in our lives. When those limits or boundaries are crossed, we have the right to seek recourse.

Prostitution is another form of sexual violence that is present in the African American community. It is rarely discussed thus an environment of collusion exist. Girls are preyed upon at young and impressionable times in their lives. Predators target them for their vulnerability and convince them they are the good guys. They are drawn into a world where on its outward appearance is filled with clothes, jewelry, money and freedom. When the truth surfaces, many are trapped in a seemingly inescapable trap. A segment of Jeanette's childhood abuse involved prostitution.

> *I was living with my father at the time. I was barely fourteen. My father, who was crack addicted allowed for a Pimp and his prostitutes to move into our home. From the moment they arrived, their mission was to make a recruit out of me. I was given access to pornography. I had never seen nor had I known so much pornography. There was garbage bag upon garbage bag of pornographic magazines. I would walk into a room and an X-rated movie would be playing. There was an instant when I walked up stairs to go to my bedroom and one of the prostitutes was massaging the Pimp with the door open. Of course, the door was intentionally left*

open. On occasion, I would awaken with strange men looking over me. I would lie there as still as I could, praying they would go away. By some miracle, they always went away.

On a hot summer evening, the Pimp asked if I wanted some new clothes. At first, I was hesitant in responding although inside I was screaming yes. My hesitance prompted him to tell his women that they were to take me shopping and buy me whatever I wanted. We arrived at the store and they immediately pointed me in the direction of short shorts and tight skirts. I was allowed to get as many as I wanted.

Later on that evening, I accompanied them on a road trip. We got on the highway and stopped at a truck stop. That was when I first witnessed a "transaction" outside of the ones that had taken place at my home. Each time they told me how easy it was and showed me the money they made. We headed back home.

When we arrived at the house, the Pimp immediately demanded that the three women give him their earnings. One by one they submitted and he counted. The third woman however, did not have an accurate amount of money. The pimp asked her for the rest of his money. After calling her multiple unsavory names, he took out his gun and put it in her vagina. He then told her, that he would pull the trigger but he didn't want to get his suit dirty. He took her outside and set her on fire. She went to the hospital and of course didn't say what happened. It was in that moment that I had become afraid.

> *Before that moment, I had contemplated becoming one of his women. It appeared that he treated them well and took care of them. I saw that was not the truth. Shortly thereafter, we lost our home. The last time I saw the Pimp was on the six o'clock news being held on unrelated charges.*

Jeanette escaped this incident physically unharmed. However, her perceptions of relationships were shaped during this period. She began to equate money and having someone share a bed as requisites in her relationships. She expected and sought out pornography. She felt the need to dress provocatively in order to attract men. The scars were invisible and deep. It would be many years before she would understand what a healthy relationship looked like. It would be many years before she could see herself as a person of value.

Redefining what a healthy relationship looks like is essential. If our thought process never changes, we will continue to get the same results. There is a lot more to a relationship than having someone pay a bill or sleeping in your bed. In a relationship, both partners have worth. They are allowed to speak freely without fear of retaliation. The words that are spoken are spoken with kindness. In a healthy relationship, if things are not working out, no one feels intimidated into staying.

A healthy relationship is created by two healthy individuals. Each person relies on themselves for happiness. Happiness within oneself allows for harmony to exist in the relationship. Being physically attracted to a person is not an indicator of a lasting relationship. While it is helpful to be attracted to your partner, it cannot be the only bond. When deciding on a partner, be aware that if they are not whole, being with you will not complete them.

Sympathy for a person will not sustain a relationship. Empathy for what that person has or is experiencing is okay. However, empathizing for a person's past pain in relationships and life is not a foundation for building a healthy bond. What they need is counseling or therapy. Without healing, the person is not in a position to be a lifelong partner.

Accepting the fact that there are people who we are not meant to enter into a relationship with can help us in making different choices. We ought to place ourselves in a position of accepting the happiness that we deserve. A person who settles for less than they deserve, will find sorrow.

It is critical for the survivor to know that she is never responsible for the abuse. An abusive person chooses to be abusive. They seek to control and rule over another. A survivor's strength in knowing who they are may be viewed as a challenge. The motive of exerting power and control over the survivor may not be revealed until well after the survivor is invested in the relationship.

We as providers must not minimize the importance of this investment to the survivor. What is important to the survivor in a relationship can be the focus of her regaining her power back. She must define what is important. We as providers have the resources to allow her to make an informed decision on what's important. Allowing ourselves to listen and gain an understanding of the survivor as a whole being places us in position to work toward change. Change in the survivor's way of thought toward her role in relationships as it relates to her culture is powerful. This change will create a ripple effect in all aspects of her life. She will feel and recognize the power that she has to be an authority in her own life.

I've been given all that one could possibly receive
Yet it is not enough
As things were given I sought more than what was due me
I continue wanting I continue taking
Yet it is not enough
Externally I seek my happiness
Approval, acceptance, attention, or gratitude
Yes gratitude!
For my mere presence in your life
Your grief is my strife
You give, I take, I take, and you give more
No matter what I do you continually open the door
Your pain is my gain
Your attempt at helping me is all in vain
For I am not happy in me
I have not loved me, known me or shown me
All the things I want from you
What I expect from you
What I think you owe me
As you give and I take
My self-destruction is the heartache you endure
As you try to ensure
That I have
And I have
All you can give
Yet it's not enough

Self Image

The way in which we view ourselves, directly impacts the way in which we view the world. One cannot disregard the importance of a positive self image. The capacity to see oneself in a positive light, allows for an ability to experience each situation on its own merit. This holds true for both service providers and survivors.

As a service provider, we are taught to take care of ourselves after a crisis has occurred. Rarely are we given specific training on recognizing the good in us as individuals. The daily trauma that can occur by dealing with the trauma of others can be overwhelming. When overwhelmed, how is possible to provide adequate service? A service provider who cannot see the positive aspects of their own lives will have a difficult time in assisting a survivor in seeing the positive aspects of receiving assistance.

Survivors are not all deplete of a positive self image. At times we can find this troubling. A survivor with a positive self image is gift. The ability to see our service provision for what it is allows us an insight into what we do well and the improvements that need to be made. It is also a starting point for us to nourish the things that we do well. This is important for growth.

For the survivors that we will work with that require

assistance in recognizing what is positive in them, we must first see it ourselves. By being culturally aware and utilizing cultural knowledge, we allow for a connection to be established with the survivor. By striving to be culturally competent in our interactions with survivors, the connections will be authentic.

Survivors are like you and I in that we have good days and some that are not so good. Survivors are our friends, neighbors, hostess, gas attendants, our bosses and our co-workers. We see them and interact with them on a daily basis, without recognizing the turmoil that may be occurring in their lives. In treating others with courtesy, dignity and respect, we are directly responsible for providing an environment where a survivor can seek services void of fear.

Working on self-image involves being in a place internally, to see it as a need and a priority. For the woman who does not have her basic needs met, such as food, clothing and shelter, this kind of work will not be on the top of the priority list. As an advocate, you will want to work towards assisting her in having her basic needs met. Once she feels that her needs are met and that she is safe and secure, the work on self-image will not seem as difficult.

To assist in construction of a positive a self-image, one must dismantle the layers that created the negative. It necessitates having a knowledge base that consists of women and African American histories in America. It consists of acknowledging how she sees herself in society today. One will have to be patient and understanding that this is not a one-hour session.

Religion and spirituality are an integral part of self-image that is often neglected by service providers. In order to avoid an offense we are silent and dismissive about the importance of faith. In our silence, many times, an offense is taken.

Survivors are people who are dealing with an issue. The issue that brought them to our door affected other aspects of their life. To be the best at our service provision, a willingness to explore their spiritual and/or religious beliefs is crucial.

Exploring a person's spiritual and/or religious belief is not complicated. Asking the survivor if they have a belief is a start. If the survivor self-discloses, being able to refer to the appropriate place of worship would be next.

Willingness to be open to a discussion about the impact of their faith on healing will open doors of trust and open honest communication. A concern for the wholeness of a person goes far beyond tolerance. A display of patience and open-mindedness for things that don't impose upon our lives reflects positively on us and our agencies. Jeannette reflects on her faith in her life.

> *During my life, I must say that had it not been for my belief in Jesus and his love for me, I may not be here today. I struggled with thoughts of suicide. I attempted suicide once. In that moment of agony and pain I prayed. I asked God to spare me. I drifted off and when I awoke, the pain was gone and I didn't feel hopeless. As for my daughter, I pray for her. I pray for her healing. She has found solace in attending bible class and hearing the sermons on Sunday. She says she feels that Jesus is speaking directly to her. I believe her because he speaks to me.*

In order to facilitate healing for survivors of color, we must acknowledge their pain. To adequately address the hurt the complacency that we have had for so long must vanish.

Acknowledging that racism in service provision exists and confronting it at a level of zero tolerance is an obligation we have to those we serve. Healing can only take place where peace and tranquility exist. Turmoil in agencies and issues ignored shape our interactions with survivors.

Allowing a place for the voices of women of color to be expressed is significant. To be a place for all women, one must visually see all women. Multicultural brochures are not enough. A survivor that comes to an agency where women of color are in leadership roles and are not silenced will believe that this may be a place where healing can occur. Leadership must be integrated at every level of the agency if it is genuine. An environment that is transparent will allow for a survivor to be open and honest. A survivor must be able to speak and be without censorship for true healing to take place.

Women of color who reach out to us for our expertise in domestic and sexual violence come with an expectation. That expectation is for us to see beyond their circumstance. The expectation is that we will see beyond all the myths and stereotypes that are circulated daily. Women of color require that we do the work to see them for who they are. Women of color who seek services should be able to reap the benefits from all the tools that we carry. That requirement, those expectations are more than reasonable.

Frequently Asked Questions

There are questions that are asked more often than others as it pertains to working with people of color. Here are some of the questions that have been asked of me including answers.

Question: I am not a racist but when a client comes in and sees that I am white, they assume that I'm racist. How do I convince them that I'm not?

Answer: It is an assumption that your clients of color assume that you are racist. Unless they have said it directly to you, this is an assumption that you cannot afford to make. Many times you are unable to convince a person of something that they can't experience for themselves. The best way to handle the situation is by doing your job and taking into consideration that person as an individual. In doing so, it will become apparent to the client the type of person they are dealing with.

Question: There is only one person of color in the agency that I work for. I go to her for every question I have on people of color and she doesn't seem to mind. Is that a problem?

Answer: Many times, people of color are placed in a position of being a dictionary for any information regarding other people of color. This is in many cases, taxing for the person.

The best way to get your information is to do your own work. It is alright to ask an occasional question for clarification, however, you don't want to marginalize the person of color.

Question: Why do we have to talk about race? I don't see color, I only see the person.

Answer: The denial of an ability to see a person's color is a denial of the ability to see an aspect of a person. That is an integral part of which they are that cannot be changed. It is a way of denying one's responsibility to achieve cultural competence. This is not a compliment to the person on the receiving end of the comment. While having a discussion on race, it is important to note that we are talking about a construct in our society used to classify groups of people. While cultural competency cannot ever be fully achieved, it is important that we continually strive for competence.

Question: Isn't it divisive to talk about service provision to people of color?

Answer: To not discuss the particular needs of a group of people is a disservice to all. The simple reality is that without a proper understanding of where a person is coming from, an offense is sure to take place. We want to eliminate those offenses whenever possible. We discuss the provision of services to people of color to fill a gap that has existed for too long. There is a change that is required in the way services are provided and we are choosing to not ignore it.

Question: Whenever I am alone with a person of color, I am afraid. I don't want to say the wrong thing so I leave my door open just in case I need help. Why is this offensive?

Answer: This is offensive to the person of color in that you are showing no regard to their right to confidentiality. While your actions may be based on past experience or misconceptions of people of color, you are sending a message that this person is not important. Take a moment and ask yourself where this fear is coming from. Take some time and work on your own issues to avoid isolating any other clients.

Question: I live in a rural area and don't come in contact with people of color, why is this important to me?

Answer: If you vacation, go to trainings, or even watch television, you are coming in contact with people of color. Unfortunately, limited contact with lack of understanding leads to more stereotypes and generalizations. It is important to seek and gain accurate information on those who do not share our same or similar backgrounds. By educating ourselves, we are armed to combat the injustices, prejudices and stereotypes that exist. Also, your neighbor may be a person of color. You cannot look at a person and accurately determine if they are a person of color or not.

Question: I have had several clients who won't work on their DV. Each time we meet they talk about the past and not the incident that brought them to me. I try to redirect and nothing works. How do I stop this from happening?

Answer: Sometimes a person just wants to be heard. The client may be testing to see if you are trustworthy. If they feel comfortable in telling you things that are not of consequence, they may later open up to you about the DV. Trust doesn't occur overnight. While you may feel as if you are spinning your wheels, listening skills are essential to the healing process of the client.

Question: When this client came to me, she was 19 with three children. Now she is 22 with six. The abuser is the same person. How can I help her if she keeps going back?

Answer: Each time she comes to you, you are dispelling a myth. The myth is that the abuser is the only one who cares for her. It is absolutely a good thing that she is comfortable in returning. Take into consideration her age and the length of the relationship with her abuser. Chances are that he has been with her before she could consent. Getting a person to realize they have other options is no easy task. Remain steadfast. You may never see what you would deem as success with her. Continue to give her support and offer strategies that will decrease her reliance on anyone other than herself.

Question: Don't we place an over-emphasis on culture? It seems to be the new trend.

Answer: Some of today's trends are culture specific. Culture itself is not a trend. Culture has been around since time itself, it is our duty to gain an understanding of our culture as well as others.

Question: My personal belief has no impact on my work, why do I have attend these types of trainings?

Answer: Our personal belief system is a part of who we are and therefore apart of our professional lives. The interactions that we have with others are a direct reflection of our belief system. For example, if you believe that pork is not good for you, the likelihood of you offering pork is slim. If the person were to be in need of something to eat, you are unlikely to give them pork. While this may seem of little consequence, your actions will be the same on major issues. For instance, if you don't believe in abortion, you probably won't feel it necessary to give information on the nearest abortion clinic. You would be more likely to refer to a clinic that is pro-life.

Question: It seems like all the people who come for services are poor. Not only are they poor, but they complain about being held back and do nothing about it. If they don't act on their own behalf, what can I possibly do for them?

Answer: Oppression occurs in many forms and is witnessed by our children on a daily basis through media images and the unfair practices in education as well as their day to day experiences in their social environment. These children grow into adults and are the people that we serve. Poverty and oppression are interrelated. These are two very important conditions in which individuals are subjected. It is a way of living that experience has taught them has no way out. Economic stability seems unattainable. The amount of assistance given by government is not enough to live on nor was it ever meant to be. The current systems today that are provided are without outside support. This may cause reliance, and at times are barriers to independence.

To combat oppression and the behaviors that are created from being oppressed, an individual must first acknowledge their condition. For an individual to acknowledge a condition, they must first know that it is present. As an advocate, you have the tools necessary to educate. Taking the time to deconstruct the myths that a client lives with in order to set them free mentally is a challenge. It is a challenge that is worth taking on.

Question: In sessions, my client speaks with crude language regarding her sexual assault. Should I try to get her to clean up her language?

Answer: A survivor must be allowed to use their own language in discussion of their assault. If the survivor is not using words that are demeaning towards you, it's a good idea to refrain from trying to correct her. Educating her on the language that is used in the materials that you will give her is a benefit as long as you don't present it in a condescending manner.

Question: Every time my client is assigned the bathroom task, she doesn't do it. It isn't fair to the other clients or the staff who are left with the responsibility of the clean up. What type of reprimand can I give?

Answer: Before you conclude that a reprimand is necessary, find out from the survivor what is it about the restroom that prevents her from cleaning it. She may not feel it necessary to clean the restroom. If this is the case, try to explain the logic behind cleaning the restroom. She may share with you that she doesn't know how to clean a restroom. If this is the case, it is solved by simply, showing her how to clean it. Be prepared. You may find out that her assault took place in a restroom and it's too painful for her to be in there any lengthy amount of time.

On the outside the survivor may appear to be handling things well. However, on the inside she may be in turmoil. In order for the survivor to feel she is able to share with us, empathetic listening is a requirement. Reassure the survivor that her healing process is going to take as long as it takes. Survivors are not going to respond to trauma in the same manner. On the surface it may appear to have occurred under a similar set of circumstances, but the uniqueness of each person makes their set of circumstances distinctive.

Question: What is an advocate's role in the journey of a survivor?

Answer: An advocate's role is to be an empathetic ear and a sound resource for connecting the survivor with agencies, information and other needs that are identified by the survivor. An advocate is non-judgmental. An advocate can listen and reflect back what has been said without jumping into problem solving. An advocate can facilitate problem solving after listening.

An advocate seeks to understand the culture of the person that is before them. The advocate is not afraid to ask questions or seek out the necessary information for proper service provision. There is recognition that the person's cultural experience is a clue into how best to provide service. The survivor is not judged on appearance or preconceived notions. The survivor is seen as the expert on her life.

Realizing that no two survivors are alike, an advocate takes the time to build a rapport with her client. An advocate recognizes the strength it takes to share with a stranger her reality, as it truly is and honors it. Patience and empathy are extended as a normal aspect of service provision.

An advocate is aware of her tools and knows how and when to use them. An advocate is not afraid to ask for clarity and does not collude with others at the detriment of the survivor. An advocate is the voice when the survivor cannot speak. She can reflect back what she has heard. The role of an advocate is to belief the survivor.

Information and Resources

➤ African American females are less likely to use services although they experience domestic violence at rates higher than their white counterparts. (Women of Color Network Facts and Stats: Domestic Violence in Communities of Color- June 2006)

➤ "Approximately 40% of Black women report coercive contact of a sexual nature by the age of 18". (Women of Color Network Facts and Stats: Domestic Violence in Communities of Color- June 2006)

➤ 1 in 12 women and 1 in 45 men have been stalked in their lifetime. (Tjaden, Patricia & Thoennes, Nancy. (1998). "Stalking in America." National Institute for Justice)

➤ Black women comprise 8% of the U.S. population but in 2005 accounted for 22% of the intimate partner homicide victims and 29% of all female victims of intimate homicide (www.ojp.usdoj.gov/bjs/homicide/intimates.htm)

➤ 85% of African Americans identify as Christian. (http://religions.pewforum.org/pdf/report-religious-landscape-study-full.pdf)2008

- ➢ Institute on Domestic Violence in the African American Community: www.dvinstitute.org

- ➢ Michigan Resource Center on Domestic and Sexual Violence: www.mcadsv.org/mrcdsv

- ➢ Family Violence Prevention Fund: www.endabuse.org

- ➢ Sisters Acquiring Financial Empowerment: www.newsafestart.org

- ➢ Faith Trust Institute: www.faithtrustinstitute.org

Acknowledgements

This book would not be possible without the support of family and friends. To my husband David, you continually encourage me to follow my dreams. Thanks for saying, "Go for it". Thank you to my brother Bryan and close friend Stephanie Hoffman-Hulbert, the two people who took the time to look at my work with a critical eye. Thank you Mom for reminding me that all the gifts that I have are from God and that without Him none of this would be possible.

I extend my appreciation to the Michigan Coalition Against Domestic and Sexual Violence Women of Color Task Force. You continue to provide a platform for the voice of women of color and for that I thank you.

My gratitude to Jeanette (name changed to protect identity) for your courage in allowing your story to be shared for the benefit of other survivors.

About the Author

Chéree Thomas is a graduate of the University of Toledo. She has been working in the field of Domestic and Sexual Violence since 1999. She has facilitated numerous trainings on DV, SA, and multiple aspects of culture and diversity. Chéree has worked as a direct service provider, supervisor and program manager. Her passion has been and continues to be assuring that people of color receive services in way that respects them as individuals. She volunteers in her community and seeks ways to serve others.

Chéree resides in the state of Michigan with her husband David and their children.

Notes

Notes

Notes

Notes

Notes

Notes

Notes

Notes

Notes

Notes

Notes

Notes

Notes

Notes

Notes

Notes

Notes